دوست است

This is bad luck

جو اُس میں کہانی ہے

Everyone has a story

ست و دو درختی را پنهان ک
اسطه پرستش کنند

Published by Marieke Slovin Lewis & Sarah Reader Harris

First published 2020 in Belgium with funding from Interlitratour
https://en.interlitratour.be/

Copyright © Marieke Slovin Lewis & Sarah Reader Harris, 2020

Printed and bound in the United States

ISBN: 978-1-7346858-0-0

Photos by authors except:
Front and back cover photos, vii, and page 49 photo by Richard S. Lewis

Page 16 photo by Erik Tys

On the Move:
Poems and Songs of Migration

Marieke Slovin Lewis

Sarah Reader Harris

Residents of Petit-Château

Dedicated to all creatures on the move

MIGRATION

Our first migration is our birth
From a muffled, velvet place
to blaring sound
and blinding light
we tumble down to earth.

The start of many lives.
Like a cat we change our coat,
wriggle out of childhood,
weather teenage blues.
Growing up is painful,
shedding skin, letting sunlight in,
turning into someone new.
We buzz around like bees. Plant seeds.
Discover different points of view.

We are creatures on the move.
It's time to spread our wings.
The geese fly north.
Butterflies head south
cross cities, mountains, seas.
There are no borders in the sky.
Painted Ladies glide so high
they leave no trace.
Reach the desert where they die.
Their young complete the trek.
No one asks them why.

Migration changes us.
We wrinkle like a walnut.
Lose pieces of ourselves, unravel
like a blanket full of holes.
There is no turning back.
The landscape too is changed.
We cannot read the signs.
Strangers become angels bearing gifts.

We travel on. Migration is our life.
Our death. We seek another country
where there's room to breathe,
the air is sweet, a scent of lemon leaves.
A door is open. Someone calls your name.

SRH

Contents

About the Project	1
About the Authors	8

Songs of Migration

Never give up	18
A peaceful life	19
The sun will come again	22
Laugh at life	23
I am the change	26
Love	27
Break the code	30
I am a word	31
Remember Rose	34
The domes of Damascus	35
If only we hope	38
Don't wait, Create	39
Nataghiar [Let's change]	42
The Pigeon song	43
Just be happy	46
I could be you, You could be me	47
Soyons unis	50
We are all human	51
Hakuna matata	54
Let me be free	55
My lovely, my lovely [Habibi, habibi]	58
The hand that hurts can also heal	59
We are the nomads	62
You're always here with me	63
Give me a chance to live	66
When you cross the border	67
A wild idea	70

About the Project: Songs of Migration

EN

Songs of Migration is a collaboration between Marieke Slovin Lewis, Sarah Reader Harris, and the residents of the Fedasil Petit-Château Arrival Centre between January 2017 and January 2020. During this time, Marieke and Sarah have been offering poetry and songwriting for the residents at the center. This creative project is an exchange of life stories. We write poems that encompass the spectrum of human experience, hopes, dreams, struggles, and emotions. We shape these poems into songs in all languages to create opportunities for cultural exchange, kinship, and welcome. There is much controversy over immigration, along with pressure for immigrants to let go of their language and customs in order to assimilate into their new home country. We believe that it is through the celebration of our diversity that we transcend fear, build empathy and understanding, and sow the seeds of solidarity. The music in this songbook represents many hours of cultural exchange, discussion, vulnerability, creativity, and love. We invite you to make these songs your own. To learn more about the writing of these songs and to listen to recordings, visit https://guidingsong.com/migrationsongs/

NL

Songs of Migration ontstonden uit een samenwerking tussen Marieke Slovin Lewis, Sarah Reader Harris, en de bewoners van het Fedasil Klein Kasteeltje Aankomst Centrum tussen januari 2017 en januari 2020. Gedurende deze periode gingen Marieke en Sarah aan de slag met poezie en muziek, mede uitgewerkt door de bewoners. Dit creatieve process is een uitwisseling van levensverhalen. Er worden gedichten geboren die het hele spectrum van menselijke ervaring, hoop, dromen, worstelingen, en emoties omvatten. De gedichten worden in liederen gegoten in vele talen zodat de mogelijkheid geschapen wordt tot uitwisseling, verwantschap, en welkom. Er is veel controverse over migratie, er is ook veel druk op binnenkomende migranten om hun taal en gebruiken los te laten zodat ze gemakkelijker in hun nieuwe thuisland kunnen assimileren. Wij geloven echter dat door onze diversiteit te erkennen, dat we angst overstijgen, empathie en begrip opbouwen, en we de zaden van solidariteit kunnen zaaien. De muziek en teksten in dit liedboek vertegenwoordigen uren van culturele uitwisseling, kwetsbaarheid, creativiteit, en liefde. We nodigen iedereen uit om je deze liederen eigen te maken. Om meer te weten te komen over de genese van de liederen en om naar fragmenten te luisteren kan je surfen naar https://guidingsong.com/migrationsongs/

FR

Songs of Migration est une collaboration entre Marieke Slovin Lewis, Sarah Reader Harris, et les résidents du centre d'accueil Fedasil Petit-Château entre janvier 2017 et janvier 2020. Pendant cette période, Marieke et Sarah ont proposé de la poésie et des chansons aux résidents du centre. Ce projet créatif est un échange de récits de vie. Nous écrivons des poèmes qui englobent le spectre de l'expérience humaine, des espoirs, des rêves, des luttes, et des émotions. Nous adaptons ces poèmes en chansons dans toutes les langues afin de créer des opportunités d'échange culturel, de lien, et d'accueil. L'immigration suscite de nombreuses controverses, et les migrants subissent beaucoup de pression pour abandonner leur langue natale et leurs coutumes afin de s'intégrer dans leur nouveau pays d'accueil. Nous pensons que c'est en célébrant notre diversité que nous transcendons la peur, que nous développons l'empathie et la compréhension et que nous semons les graines de la solidarité. La musique de ce recueil de chansons représente de nombreuses heures d'échanges culturels, de discussions, de vulnérabilité, de créativité, et d'amour. Nous vous invitons à vous approprier ces chansons. Pour en savoir plus sur l'écriture de ces chansons et pour écouter les enregistrements, visitez le site https://guidingsong.com/migrationsongs/

About the Authors:

Marieke Slovin Lewis, Sarah Reader Harris, Residents of Petit-Château

Marieke Slovin Lewis

EN

Marieke is originally from the United States. She composes music by shaping a story into a song, using a method of songwriting she calls Story-to-Song (STS). She writes music with individuals and groups, facilitating the creative process so a song may reveal itself in its own unique way, be it from a spoken story, written words or phrases, or a poem. The creation of each song is unique to those who participate in the process. Marieke holds a PhD in Sustainability Education and works as an editor, writer, yoga instructor, and musician. To learn more about Marieke, visit: www.mariekeslovin.com

NL

Marieke komt oorspronkelijk uit de Verenigde Staten. Ze componeert muziek door een verhaal tot een lied om te vormen. Ze gebruikt daarbij een methode die ze STS (Story-to-Song) noemt. Ze creeërt muziek met zowel individuen als met groepen. Daarbij faciliteert ze het creatieve proces zodat het lied op een eigen unieke manier tevoorschijn komt. Vertrekpunt kan zowel een verhaal dat mondeling overleverd, wordt zijn als een geschreven tekst of gezegden of een gedicht. Marieke heeft een doctoraat in Duurzame Educatie en werkt als redacteur, yoga-lerares, en muzikant. Om meer te weten over Marieke, kan je surfen naar www.mariekeslovin.com

FR

Marieke est originaire des États-Unis. Elle compose la musique en transformant une histoire en chanson, en utilisant une méthode d'écriture qu'elle appelle Story-to-Song (STS). Elle écrit de la musique de manière individuelle ou en groupe, facilitant le processus créatif afin qu'une chanson puisse se révéler à sa manière, qu'elle provienne d'une histoire parlée, de mots ou de phrases écrites, ou d'un poème. La création de chaque chanson est propre à chaque personne qui participe à son processus. Marieke est titulaire d'un doctorat en éducation au développement durable et travaille en tant que rédactrice, écrivaine, professeur de yoga, et musicienne. Pour en savoir plus sur Marieke, visitez: www.mariekeslovin.com

Sarah Reader Harris

EN

Originally from the UK, Sarah has been living in Belgium for the past several decades. She writes children's books, some of which have been translated into Dutch and French, and she organizes storytelling sessions and educational projects based on these stories. To learn more about these books visit www.asheepcalledskye.com Sarah is a member of the Brussels Writers Circle and her short stories and poems have been published in various anthologies. She works with asylum seekers and as a guardian for unaccompanied minors and regularly organizes open mic evenings in CEDES house in Brussels.

NL

Sarah komt oorspronkelijk uit het VK maar leeft al tientallen jaren in België. Ze schrijft kinderboeken in het engels, waarvan sommige vertaald zijn in het nederlands en het frans. Ze is ook een verhalenverteller en begeleidt educatieve werkwinkels die gebaseerd zijn op haar verhalen. Om meer te weten te komen over haar boeken, kan je surfen naar www.asheepcalledskye.com. Sarah is een lid van de Brussels Writers Circle en haar kortverhalen en gedichten werden gepubliceerd in verschillende anthologieën. Ze werkt bij en met asielzoekers en is voogd van niet begeleide minderjarigen. Regelmatig organiseert ze Open Mic avonden in het CEDES huis in Brussel.

FR

Originaire du Royaume-Uni, Sarah vit en Belgique depuis plusieurs décennies. Elle écrit des livres pour enfants, dont certains ont été traduits en néerlandais et en français, et elle organise des séances de contes et des projets éducatifs basés sur ces histoires. Pour en savoir plus sur ces livres, visitez www.asheepcalledskye.com Sarah est membre du Brussels Writers Circle et ses nouvelles et poèmes ont été publiés dans diverses anthologies. Elle travaille avec des demandeurs d'asile et en tant que tutrice de mineurs non accompagnés et organise régulièrement des soirées open mic dans la maison CEDES à Bruxelles.

Residents of Petit-Château

EN

Every one of the songs in this book was written with asylum seekers who came to Brussels, Belgium in search of a better, safer life. The lyrics were born from spoken and written words and phrases that convey the story of their journeys, hopes, dreams, fears, and sadness. There are songs from Macedonia, Gaza, Palestine, Syria, Eritrea, Iraq, Iran, Afghanistan, Poland, Romania, Gambia, Burundi, Senegal, Yemen, Turkey, Azerbaijan, Armenia.

NL

Elk van de liederen in dit boek werden geschreven met asielzoekers die naar Brussel, België, kwamen op zoek naar een beter, veilig leven. De teksten werden geboren vanuit de woorden en uitdrukkingen die het verhaal van hun tochten, hoop, dromen, angsten en droefheid weergeven. Er zijn liederen vanuit Macedonië, Gaza, Palestina, Syrië, Eritrea, Irak, Afghanistan, Polen, Roemenië, Gambië, Burundi, Senegal, Yemen, Azerbeijan, Armenië.

FR

Chacune des chansons de ce livre a été écrite avec des demandeurs d'asile venus à Bruxelles, en Belgique, à la recherche d'une vie meilleure et plus sûre. Les paroles sont nées de mots et de phrases parlés et écrits qui transmettent l'histoire de leurs voyages, espoirs, rêves, peurs, et tristesse. Il y a des chansons de Macédoine, Gaza, Palestine, Syrie, Érythrée, Irak, Iran, Afghanistan, Pologne, Roumanie, Gambie, Burundi, Sénégal, Yémen, Turquie, Azerbaïdjan, Arménie.

NON AUX CENT

NIEMAND IS ILLEGAAL

Songs of Migration

Everyone wants to be your
نوخدل جوابس وبرابن
When you have something they want

⇒ In life there are second chances
Some people, they live in the past
they don't want to live today
they think too much and they are alone
they don't move forward   Amazing Life
You make new friends   Nolosha wayaab
                        Marba wax bey ku
⇒ You can start again   tustaa

~~████████████████████~~

⇒ Never give up. Life is here & now
                                    تو بیو نش کی ایل ات
You never know how long you will live
so it's better to be kind to one another
                                    ماس ای باش یل جا ابل تا

Never give up
Afghanistan, Key of Am

CHORUS
Am
In life [Sing this line only for the first chorus]
            D
There are second chances
Am   D
You can start again
            Am   D
Never give up, Never give up
E   Am
[Pause] Life is here and now
*Repeat Chorus

Some people, they live in the past
They don't want to live today
They think too much, and they are alone
They don't know
Life is here and now

CHORUS

You never know how long you will live
So be kind to everyone
Believe in your dream, believe in your dream
And you will see
Life is here and now

CHORUS

Don't worry about yesterday
Tomorrow isn't far away
You can fix your mistakes
It will all be ok, if you can say
Life is here and now

CHORUS

(Dari)
Am
            زندگی شانس دووم دارد
Zendagi shans dowom darad
D
            زندگی شانس دووم دارد
Zendagi shans dowom darad
Am
            زندگی شانس دووم دارد
Zendagi shans dowom darad
D   E
            زندگی شانس دووم دارد
Zendagi shans dowom darad
                  Am
Life is here and now

A peaceful life
Chorus from Macedonia and verses from other countries, Key of C

CHORUS
```
         Am      G         C
```
I want a peaceful life for my children
```
         Am      G         C
```
I want a peaceful life for myself
```
F                      C
```
No more change, no more stress
```
                 G
```
No more moving around
```
Am   G         C  F
```
I want a peaceful life
```
Am   G         C
```
I want a peaceful life

```
C
```
I crossed an ocean to get here with 500 other people
```
       F           C            G
```
I lost 20 of my friends but somehow I survived
```
Dm          Am
```
Now I am here, far from the life I've known
```
Dm              G
```
And I'll never give up hope

CHORUS

I fell in love with a man
I went against my family
So I left home
And I've been moving ever since
We've lived on the street
My three little boys and me
I just want us to be happy

CHORUS

I came here on my own
I left my mother and my aunt
I've been living at the asylum center
For two months and a year
I want them to join me
But they're afraid of what they don't know
I'm tired of living here alone

CHORUS

L'EXCLUSION N'EST PAS UNE SOLUTION

The sun will come again
Palestine, Key of A

A
I came from Palestine to live a new life
D A E
I was alone I didn't know when I would see you
 D A
It's hard for me to see your pain
D E
I want to see you smile again

CHORUS
 A D A
So hold me, take me, fix me, I'm broken
F#m D A
Love me, heal me, the sun will come again
 D A
The sun will come again

We can fly like birds
See life from another side
The door is open wide
And nothing will be closed
It's hard for me to see your pain
I want to see you smile again

CHORUS

Laugh at life
Gaza, Key of Am

CHORUS
```
       F              Am
Laugh at life, and life laughs back
       E              Am
Laugh at life, and life laughs back
```
(Arabic)
```
             F         Am
```
اضحك للدنيا تضحكلك

Edhak le aldonya, tedhaklak
```
             E         Am
```
اضحك للدنيا تضحكلك

Edhak le aldonya, tedhaklak

```
         F         E
When life closes in all around me
         Am       E      Am
I feel smaller and smaller and smaller
F                 G
And all of a sudden it's open
         Am       E      Am
And I breathe, and I live, and I love
```

CHORUS

When darkness falls all around me
And I can't see a path to take
Slowly the dawn awakens
And I breathe, and I live, and I love

CHORUS

When life gives you a reason to be sad
Show life you have a reason to smile
The dawn will always awaken
So I breathe, and I live, and I love

CHORUS

```
Am     E  Am
Laugh at life
```

إضحك للدنيا تضحكلك

Laugh ~~at that~~ at Life and
the life will laugh ~~ba~~ for ~~to~~ you

Edhak Le Al donya Tedhaklak
(laugh)   (life)   (life laugh back
                          for you)

Laugh at life   } Refrain
And life laughs back

ضاقت وملا إستحكمت حلقاتها فرجت
وكنت أظنها لا تفرج

When life closes in all around me
   it gets smaller + smaller + smaller
and then all of a sudden it's open
and I breathe + I live + I love

When darkness falls all around me
   and I can't see any path to take
then slowly the day awakens

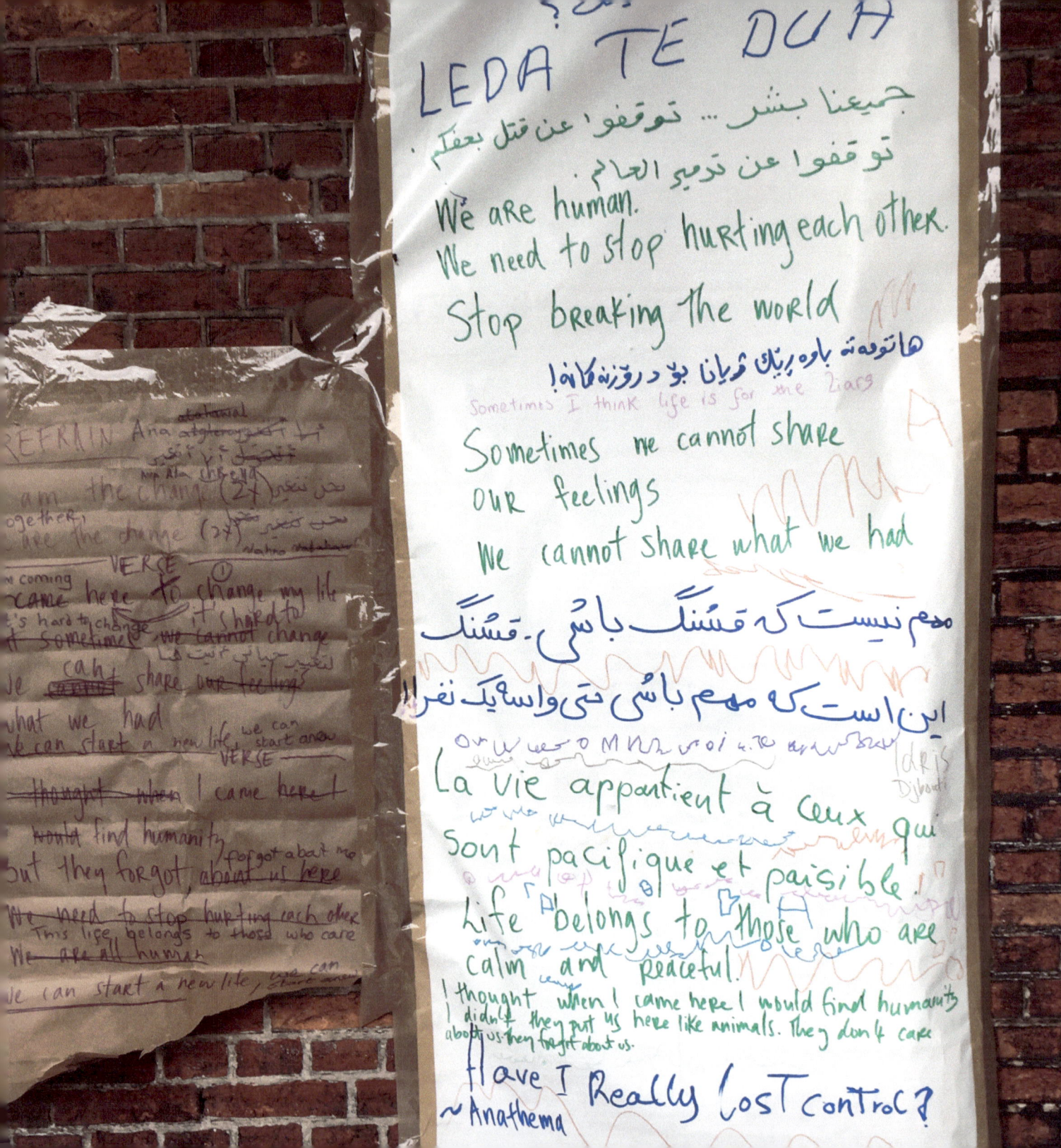

I am the change
Gaza, Key of G

CHORUS
```
       G                D
I am the change, I am the change
  Am            C
Together, we are the change
```
(Arabic)
```
       G                D
```
أنا التغيير أنا التغيير
'ana altaghyir, 'ana altaghyir
```
        Am          C
```
سويا نحن التغيير
Sawiaan nahn altaghyir
```
       G
```
نحن التغيير
Nahn altaghyir

To change my life, I'm coming here
It's hard to change, but we have to change
We can share what we have
We can start a new life, we can start anew

CHORUS

I came here to find humanity
But they forgot, they forgot about me
This life belongs to those who care
We can start all over, we can go from here

```
       G                D
I am the change, I am the change
  Am            C
Together, we are the change
```

(Arabic)
```
         G                D
```
أنا التغيير أنا التغيير
'ana altaghyir, 'ana altaghyir
```
          Am          C
```
سويا نحن التغيير
Sawiaan nahn altaghyir

(Nederlands)
Ik ben de verandering, ik ben de verandering
Samen, zijn we de verandering

(français)
Je suis le changement, je suis le changement
Tous ensemble, nous sommes le changement

```
             G                D
I am the change, I am the change
  Am            C
Together, we are the change
             G
We are the change
```

Love
Afghanistan, Key of Am

CHORUS
(Dari)
```
        Am              E
```
عشق جوری است که تو زندگی میکنی
Ish chetor zindagi kardan ast
```
        Am              F
```
عشق چیزی است که تو انجام میدی
Ish cheesiest ka to anjam midi
```
        C               E
```
چیزی خوبی انجام میدی
To yak kave khobi mikoni
```
        Am    E    Am
```
و این همان عشق است
Wa ishk eesh namin ast

Love is how you live
Love is what you do
You do something good
And that is love, too

CHORUS

Life is much too short
We have to carry on
The only ship there is
Is the ship we are all on

CHORUS
And that is love, too

qui nous fait tous bouger dans le même sens
nous révèlent le bon endroit sur lequel on se
dirige.

We are الابارجان مخر داردجدای

نوبال کسم داردمبدای

We are all on the same ship
but we have different futures

Chorus:
Love is how you live,
Love is what you do
You do something good
And that's love too.

~~Allah yar jan cheter~~

Ishk chetor ~~cheter~~ sindgi kar dan āst
Ishk ~~chetor~~ cheesie āst ka to anjam midi
Yak karv
to ~~cheesie mikoni~~ khobe mikoni

wa Ishk ma hamin hast

Ishk chetor Zindagi kardan ast
Ishk cheesiest ka to anjam midi
ta Yak kare khobi mikoni
wa Ishk hamin ast

Life is زندگی too short

کمی برایش. کار کنید.
We have to move on...

Break the code
Iran, Key of Am

```
Am            G      Am
How do I break the code and sing?
            G    D
I need somebody to explain
   Am          G       E
I want someone to share my pain
     Am         G      Am
Without my kids I'm not the same
```

CHORUS (2x)
```
     C    G
The past is past
       D   Am
I'm an optimist
     C    G    D
The best is yet to come
```
* Second time end on Am

I'm an immigrant from a foreign land
I've been there, too, I understand
Come walk with me, we'll make a stand
Heart to heart and hand in hand

CHORUS (2x)

I am a word
Syria, Gaza, Key of G

       G
I am a word of hope and love
       D
I bring honor to the world
       Am
I will push the darkness away
       C
Can I come to your house and stay?
       G
I am a word

I am the root of all resistance
I bring light for us to grow
I will push the sorrow away
Can I come to your heart and stay?
I am a word

I am the life you've left behind
The path that you now follow
The melody of your song
The place you can belong

I am a word of hope and love
I bring honor to the world
I will push the darkness away
Can I come to your house and stay?
I am a word

فلسطين
is alive

Home is where my soul lives/belongs

Come back, come back, everything you
If muslim, christian, whatever you are—c
This door is not for despair, a
Ah 100 times if you broken your promise 100 times
Come back, come back, come back

BA

Baza - Baza -

سلام منى
سراقب
Saraqib
2018

أنا الشهيدة شهد أحب الورد!
قتلني الطيران السوري
والروسي وقتلوا معي أبي

Rose – Killed in Syria – Rest in peace
9 years old with her father

I am a martyr
witnessed

Remember Rose
she's 9 years old
she never lived to tell you this

Remember Rose
Syria, Afghanistan, Key of Am

CHORUS
(Arabic)
Am   C   Am   C
أنا الشهيدة   أنا الشهيد
'ana alshahidat 'ana alshahid
Am   C
أنا الشهيد
'ana alshahid
   G
  انا
'ana

Remember Rose, she's nine years old
She never lived to tell you this
Remember Rose, she's nine years old
Killed by the bombs in Saraqib

CHORUS

Come back, come back, everything you are
Muslim, Christian, whatever you are
If you broke your promise one hundred times
Come back, I will be here

CHORUS

(Dari)
Am   C
برگرد   برگرد
Bazay, bazay, come back, come back (3x)
(Arabic)
G   Am
  انا
'ana

The domes of Damascus
Syria, Key of Am

   Am   E
I love you, dear
Am   D
I love you with your head held high
        F   E
Like the domes of Damascus
       F   E
Like the minarets of Egypt
                 Am
Like the desert of Algeria

(Arabic)
F   G
أحبك حبيبي
'ahbak habibi, I love you
F   D
أحبك حبيبي
'ahbak habibi
  Am
I love you

Achobek

I love you dear

أحبك أيتها الغالية

I love you with your head high lik[e]
the domes of Damascus

قبابُ دمشق

Like the minarets of Eg[ypt]
مآذن مصر

Like the desert of Algeria
الصحراء الجزائري

ALMOSABA

Bhebk Habibi
Hebek I lov[e]

ኩሉ ያሕልፍ፡ all will pass
Culu yhalif

ፍቕሪ ግን ይተርፍ፡፡ but love will stay
Fiqri gn jtrf

ኣብ ናይ ሕወት ሕልሚ፡ In the dream of life
Ab Nai Gwat Helmi

ኩሉ ጋሕዲ ይኾነ፡፡ everything will come true
Culu Gahadi You

ተስፋ ጥራይ፡፡ only we hope
Tesfa Tri   only we hope

Un homme sans amis
C'est comme une fleur sans odeur

If only we hope
Eritrea, Key of A

CHORUS
```
A       E       F#m      D
All will pass, but love will stay
A       E       D       A
Only we hope, if only we hope
        A       E       F#m        D
In the dream of life, everything will come true
A       E       D       A
Only we hope, if only we hope
```

(Tigrinya)
```
E
ኩሉ ነገር ይሓልፍ
Kulu yhalif
          A
ፍቅሪ ግን ከጸንሕ ይኽእል
Fkri gin yterif
     E
ኣብ ሕልሚ ሓልሚ ውሽጢ
Ab nay hiwet
              A
ኩሉ ነገር ሓቂ እዩ
Kulu gahdi eyu
         D        E
ሕጉስ ኩን, ሕጉስ ኩን
Tesfa tray, tesfa tray
```

CHORUS

(français)
Un homme sans amis, c'est comme une fleur sans odeur
La souffrance corrige mieux que le conseil
Ils vous aiment, vous mêmes
Et dieu vous aime aussi

CHORUS
* Repeat last line

Don't wait, Create
Iraq, Key of Am

      Am
How hard it is to love someone
      Dm   F
When you've been left behind
Dm   F   G
This is your life, don't let others live it for you
Am   Dm   F
I have lived beautiful days and learned many things
Dm   F   G
I love good people, and I love you very much

CHORUS (2x)
     Am
Don't wait, don't wait
   F   G
Create, create

(español)
Quiero vivo como el mundo
A life in this world
Toda la vida en el momento
*Repeat

CHORUS

Some wait for hope, some wait for life, for opportunity
They don't live now, they don't seize the day
Don't wait for love, don't wait for hope, for opportunity
Live your life now, live it for today

CHORUS
     Am
Don't wait

Nataghiar [Let's change]
Gaza, Key of Dm

```
Dm                      A
We are human, we are the same
        Dm              A
We are human, and we can change
        Gm
We can have a better life
        A
If we celebrate our divide
Gm                              A
Don't close your mind to life, let's change
```

Life is beautiful, enjoy your life
Life is beautiful, free your mind
You can have a better life
If you celebrate our divide
Open your mind to life and change

(Arabic)

نحن بشر ، متساوون

Nahn bashar, mutsawun

نحن بشر ، نتغير

Nahn bashar, nataghiar
We can have a better life
If we celebrate our divide
Don't close your mind to life, let's change
```
        Dm
```
نتغير

Nataghiar

The Pigeon song
Eritrea, Key of D

```
D              A
I am a bird with a broken wing
    Bm              G
But I'm still learning how to sing
D              A
Nobody likes me, nobody loves me
    Bm          G
But still I sing every day
```

CHORUS
```
         D        A
All I have is this moment
    Bm      G
All I have is this time
D        A       G
We are not so different, you and I
         D       A
Let us share this moment
    Bm      G
Let us share this time
D        A          D
We are not so different, you and I
```

I woke up this morning
And I could not hear my song
But somehow I found a way to carry on

CHORUS

When my song is hard to find
Will you share your song with me?
If we sing together, we create harmony

CHORUS

dog
cat I am

I am a bird with a broke[n]
But I'm still learning how to sing
Nobody still know how
Nobody likes me nobody loves
But still I live every day
all I have
All I have is this moment
All I have is this time
We are not so different, you
Let us share this mom[ent]
Let us share this ti[me]
We are not so different,

I woke up this morning a[nd]
I could not hear my son[g]
Bu[t]

ere must be a place for me

"ፖርዓ ሣ፯ ሟነቶ · ፍፖረ · ህዞዳሃ፯ ዝ.ዩ፡፡"

· The meaning of life is To be happy. and give Love no matter who are u and where from,... Just be happy...(2)

Just be happy
Eritrea, Key of F

```
F            C         Dm
The meaning of life is to be happy
         C          F
And to give love to everyone
         C          Dm          C
No matter who you are or where you come from
        F C Dm C
Just be happy
        F C Dm C
Just be happy
```

The sun travels behind the horizon
Without crossing any borders
The world should not be a prison with borders
Just be happy, just be happy

The world is open to everyone
For everyone to give love
No one stop me from happily living beneath the sun
Just be happy, just be happy

```
        F        C
Stop crying, stop thinking
        Dm       C
Just be happy, just be happy
```
*Repeat 3x

```
      F
Be happy
```

I could be you, You could be me
Gaza, Key of F

CHORUS
F
I could be you, you could be me
                                        C
We can change the dark to light if we want to be free
Bflat   C   F   Bflat
We are bound together if only we could see
F   C   F
I could be you, you could be me

We don't choose our species if we're a peacock or a pigeon
We don't choose our family, our country, or religion
I could be the king of Belgium, he could be a refugee
I could be you, you could be me

What if we couldn't see the color of our skin
All we could see was the person's soul within
Buddhist, Christian, Jewish, Shiite, or Sunni
I could be you, you could be me

We don't have to follow a story born of fear
We all come from somewhere else, but we're together here
Our fate is not yet written, it's who we choose to be
I could be you, you could be me

CHORUS
*Sing last line 3x (play Bflat in between and end on F)

Soyons unis
Africa, Key of Am

    Am
Treasure the moment
     E
Even if it's small
G
Smile for everyone
    D
It's the same earth for us all
    Am
Life is fleeting
    D
We are all on the same boat
    G
From this earth we arrive
    E
And from this land we go

CHORUS
(francais)
  F
Soyons unis
   C
Ce n'est que la vie
E
Nous sommes ensemble
Am
Together, you and me
F
Ici nous arrivons
C
Ici nous partirons
E
Nous sommes ensemble
Am
We must carry on

This is our life
This is our earth
This is our death
And this is our birth

You can't take it with you
You cannot stop the tide
So let us go together
On this sometimes stormy ride

CHORUS

BRIDGE (2x)
Am
Together we laugh
Together we cry
E
Together we live
Together we die
D
Together we warm
Together we freeze
Am
Together we're trapped
Together we're free

CHORUS
*Repeat last line

We are all human
Gaza, Key of Am

Intro Am Dm G (2x)

CHORUS
```
Am         Dm
We are all human
         G          Am
We all have the same blood
              Dm  G
We are tired from war
Am                Dm
We want to live in peace
            G        Am
It doesn't matter who you are
          E
You are human

G                         Am
There was a beautiful time long ago
              E
When we lived in peace together
G
Now we've lost everything
Am
Palestine and Israel
E                   Am
Politics make us miserable
```

CHORUS

Each year they give us a short peacetime
Then war comes back again
There is no fighting for one month, maybe two
Then rockets fly every time

CHORUS

BRIDGE
```
Dm
We have no means to live in Gaza
                  Am
We come to Belgium to live a new life
                Dm
I brought my family here to make a new start
                Am
I want my son to grow up without hate in his heart
```

(Arabic) (Hebrew)
E
سلام سلام شלום שלום
Salaam, Shalom, Salaam, Shalom

Interlude Am Dm G (2x)

CHORUS
```
        Am
We are human
```

Rien ne vaut l'Amour!

I'm from Gaza

I Love you belgium

We are Palestinias

We losted all every thing.

every year they give us a short peace time when there is no fighting for a month 2 months and when we see the peace and the beautiful life, then the war comes back again

sahir from gaza

We have no means to live in Gaza.
we come here to have a good, peaceful life
politics make our life miserable
and we are tired from war.

We are all human
We all have the same blood
we are tired from war
we want to live in peace, together
it doesn't matter who you are
Palestinian Jewish
you are human

(margin: there was a beautiful time when we lived in peace together (long time) Palestine and Israel)

CHORUS: TOSHIKANE MIKOTO
TUTAFIR SA

Hakuna matata
Burundi, Senegal, Afghanistan, Key of A
In memory of Buddy

CHORUS
(Swahili)
```
    A     D    F#m   E
Hakuna Matata
       A     D    F#m   E
Tushikane Mikono
       A     D    F#m
Tutafika Salama
     E    A    D    F#m
Nabila Silah
     E    A    D    F#m   E
Nabila Silah
```

If they opened the borders, opened the borders
Where would everybody go?
Like a bird, no pain, no visa
Just the power of our wings
and our hearts to decide

CHORUS

If they opened the borders, opened the borders
Where would you go?
Would you choose one place or migrate?
I would make a new life in Belgium

CHORUS

BRIDGE
C#m
But even a bird can be hunted
There is danger in the sky
(français)   (Swahili)
A
Petit à petit, polé polé

Give us the freedom to decide
D
Hand in hand, *main dans la main*
    E
En paix on arrive, in peace we land
Peace is our land

CHORUS

(Dari)
زندگی آرام داشته باشیم
Zindagy aram dashta bashim
Relax, live for all time

(Wolof)
Africa la diougidé, Ñieuw
Fekk finiou diougidé founé

(français)
Si tu savais à quel point tu me manques
Combien je pense à toi

Interlude D E (2x)

    D   E
I come from Africa, and I find the whole world
    D   E
Africa
           A
Hakuna Matata

Let me be free
Armenia, Key of A

CHORUS
```
     A              D
Let me be free, free like a smile
          F#m       E
Free from your judgment of me
      A           D
Let me be free like an idea
           F#m   E
Free from your fear of me
```

I'm searching for an identity
That isn't based on nationality
What could it be? Would we be free?
If we let go of all our xenophobia

CHORUS

I am a person without a promised land
I am looking for someone who will understand
Could it be you? Can you see me?
Can we take charge of our destiny?

CHORUS

BRIDGE (A D F#m E until *)
Let me be free, free from what
Free from whom, free to be
Free for you, free for me
It's a complicated history
Those with power, they decide
But freedom comes from inside
Do you have a dream of what freedom could be?
Stop and think, what is freedom actually?
Free to go here, free to go there
Not be judged by the color of our…hair

For as long as there's people
There's this need to control
But the essence of nature is about letting go
We hang onto structures, systems, and rules
Build a wall around ourselves, we listen to fools
A border has two sides, but which side is safe
If we create separation, mistrust, and hate?
```
*    A                    D
The only way forward is to embrace…
     F#m
The chaos, the calm
The difference, the same
     E
The heartbeat, the bloodshed
Inhuman, humane
     F#m
The daybreak, the nightfall
Beginning and end
E
Everything, nothing
Enemy, friend
```

Am I alone or are you also trying
To be free from who they want you to be?
Could we agree and disagree
And find a way to live in harmony?

CHORUS
```
          A           E         A
Let us be free, we could try it, and see
```

ARMENIA

Սասցած բոլորին պահպան
Դպիրտ թող աանդապաշ լինի
Անկախ ազգային
պատկանելության։

:)

God bless everybody
Let the smile always be
 independent of nationality

We are not here
We are not there
We are somewhere inbetween

I am ~~not~~ you
I am ~~not~~ ~~there~~
I am somew[here]

my lovely,
Where is the tim[e]
my lovely, my lo[vely]
I am somewhere in[between]
my lovely, my lov[ely]
Can you meet me on [the]
my lovely, my lovely, I [want] to
my lovely, my lovely, Can you meet me in the sky?
my lovely, my we will have to travel to sky
lovely.

Nahnu Laissa Hena
نحن لسنا هنا
نحن لسنا هناك
Nahnu ~~Laisa~~
Nahnu Wak AL Buad Kochu
Fe Ma[
Ana L~~ysso~~ Ante
Ana L~~ysso~~ Ana
Ana Boina Albad

My lovely, my lovely [Habibi, habibi]
Palestine, Key of G

```
    G           D
My lovely, my lovely
            Am          Em
Where is the time we used to meet?
    G           D
My lovely, my lovely
        Am            Em
I am somewhere in between
```

My lovely, my lovely
Will you meet me on the moon?
My lovely, my lovely
I need to see you soon

My lovely, my lovely
Will you meet me in the sky?
My lovely, my lovely
We will have to learn to fly

(Arabic)
حبيبي ، حبيبي
Habibi, habibi
سنلتقي في القمر
Sanaltaqi fi alqamar

حبيبي ، حبيبي
Habibi, habibi
أحتاج لقياك
Ahtaj liqiak

حبيبي ، حبيبي
Habibi, habibi
أنا أنت أنت أنا
'ana 'ant ant ana

حبيبي ، حبيبي
Habibi, habibi
أنا بين قبلك
'ana bayn qablik

حبيبي ، حبيبي
Habibi, habibi
بحبك سوى أنتم عمري
Bihbik siwaa 'antum eumri

The hand that hurts can also heal
Gaza, Poland, Romania, Key of A

Em
Enough with all the hate
A
Away with all the prejudice
    Em
It's time for a change
   A
But how?

We've been living upside down
The choice is in our hands
We can turn the world around
But how?

I want to feed the birds
See the world anew
Put our differences aside
Try another point of view
With you

How can I know that you are real?
How can I feel what you feel?
Can I take you by the hand?
The hand that hurts can also heal

Picture an abandoned child
In a corner all alone
It's dark and it's cold
There's no way home

Put your arms around me
Take me from this hopeless place
Are you a stranger or someone else?

Come and find me
You could be my light and hope
                          B7
Are you a stranger or really my own Self?
                 Em
How can I know that you are real?
              A
How can I feel what you feel?
                 Em
How can I know that you are real?
              A
How can I feel what you feel?
Em
The hand that hurts can also heal
A   Em
[Pause] Can also heal

Enough with all the hate
Away with all the prejudice
It's time for a change
But how?

Tired of living upside down
The choice is in our hands
We can turn the world around
But how?

I want to feed the birds
See the world anew
Put our differences aside
Try ~~Have~~ another point of view
with you

How can I see that you are real?
How can I feel what you feel?
Can I take you by the hand?
The hand that hurts can also heal

Picture an abandoned child
In a corner all alone
It's dark and it's cold
There's no way home
Put your arms around me
Take me from this hopeless place
Are you a stranger or
 someone else?
Come & find me

We are the nomads
Turkey, Key of Am

```
            Am      E
We are the nomads
               Am
Who stole our war?
                Dm
We are the nomads
E        Am
You stole our war
```

We are free spirits
Not bound by rules
We are the natives
You experiment with our souls

```
       Am      E      D      E
Our souls and our bodies are not yours to define
       Am      E      D      E
The beauty of war we use to defy
Am      E      D         E
We go to war to protect who we are
       Am      E
But you stole our war machine
              Am
And turned it against us
```

We are the nomads
Who stole our war?
We are the nomads
You stole our war

You're always here with me
Azerbaijan, Key of Am

```
        Am
It's been three long years
        D
My eyes are full of tears
Am              D
I cannot look at your picture
C           D
As a refugee, I live uncertainty
             E
But you're always here with me
         Am
In my heart
```

I've tried three different times
In three different countries
But still I have no answer
There are words I can say
To help us through the day
You're always here with me in my heart

The things that make us sad
Can also bring us joy
This is what life is about
As a refugee, I live uncertainty
But you're always here with me in my heart
          E   Am
You're always here with me in my heart

Give me a chance to live
Yemen, Key of F

CHORUS
```
      Bflat      Dm
I don't come to take
   C       F
I come to live
Bflat       Dm       C
Give me a chance to give
       Bflat      Dm
I ran away from war
      C       F
To feel human again
Bflat       Dm       C
Give me a chance to live
```

```
           F              C
I'm from Yemen, I lost my life there
           Dm
My parents' bodies were broken
     C
By bombs from the war
           F               C
It's been two years away from my country
            Dm              C
My mom and dad they're waiting for me
```

```
C                         Dm
Before the war I was working to help my family
         Bflat              C
It was a hard life, but we were safe
C                   Dm
If Belgium will give me a chance to live
Bflat                  C
[Pause] I will give her everything
```

CHORUS

I spent a month and a half on the street in Spain
I saw the real face of refugees
The police there told me to go to hell
So I took a bus and crossed the border
Into Belgium from France

I saw a policeman and thought, he'll tell me to go to hell
He took out his phone and waved to me
He said, welcome, and he showed me a place to stay
He saw the human being in me

CHORUS

BRIDGE
```
           Dm                  C
When I was 14, I'd say to my friends
                          Bflat
Nothing's impossible in life
                   Dm
But then the war came
Dm                  C
Life is hard when you're alone
                  Bflat         Dm
I live like I'm a hundred without hope
       C
To Belgium, I say thank you
                           Dm
You've given me the shoes on my feet
              Bflat             C
and I want to show my gratitude
   C                Dm
Let me live in here, safe and free
Bflat                    C
[Pause] See the human being in me
```

CHORUS
```
            F
Give me a chance
```

When you cross the border
Gambia, Key of Dm

CHORUS
Dm
Africa, it's a long story
'cross checkpoints and desert
     A
Over land and sea
     Dm   F   Bflat
From Gambia to Belgium, by way of Italy
Dm   C   F C
When you cross the border, you are free
Dm   C   Dm
When you cross the border, you are free

     Dm
I went from Gambia to Senegal to Mali Burkina Faso
     A
Took the back way into Libya to avoid getting caught
Bflat
Across the Sahara 'neath the desert sun in a pickup truck
     A
At every checkpoint you have to pay
Or they turn you away

CHORUS

If you go to Tripoli and say I want to go to Italy
They say go to this man and hide from the police
From Tripoli by boat is 10 hours
From Zuwara four or five
It's cold, you can't drink, you can't lie down
You're lucky if you survive

CHORUS

In Italy they stare at you if you are black
You don't get respect
They tell you to go back
I tried five years for asylum, and I got a negative
But I won't go back to Africa
I've seen how other people live

CHORUS

BRIDGE
Bflat
Across the border into France
     F
I hid in the toilet on the train
     C
Across the border into Belgium
     F
I hid in there again
     Bflat
You suffer to get here
And when you finally arrive
     A
You don't choose if you can stay
Someone else gets to decide

CHORUS

All We Need is Love ♡

A wild idea
Belgium, Key of D

```
D
Here's an idea, a wild idea
                        A
What if we opened the door?
What a pleasure to meet you
We're on our way to
                    D
A place without any walls
```

CHORUS
(français)
```
G       D
Pas de porte, pas de passeport
G              D
We are all passing through
G       F#m      G
Pas de porte, pas de passeport
        A        D
Can I open the door for you?
```

Here's an idea, a wild idea, anyone can begin
It doesn't take much, a smile a touch
To let the stranger in

CHORUS

Here's an idea, a wild idea
Every person is somebody's child
Another idea, a wilder idea
Every person is everyone's child

CHORUS

BRIDGE
```
F#m
Why can't I go where I want to go?
Why do you close the door?
          D
If we're all worth the same then why is your life
Worth so much more?
G                                D
Come into the space where you can breathe
G              D
See the world anew
G
We're in it together, breathe the same air
        A
I can share this world with you
```

So, here's an idea, a wild idea
These words can change the world
                      (Nederlands)
You are welcome, *welgekomen*
Will you come in?
(German)   (français)
Willkommen, bienvenue

CHORUS
* Repeat last line

THANK YOU FOR COMING

For all asylum seekers

Thank you for coming
for crossing dangerous seas
to build your future here
with the likes of you and me.

Thank you for coming
for being who you are
with your languages, your customs,
you who seek another star.

Thank you for coming
for brightening our days,
not with myrrh and gold and frankincense,
but the chance to change our ways.

It's not the places that we come from
but the future that we make,
not the borders that enclose us
but the walls we choose to break.

So thank you for coming
for giving us a hand
in making little Belgium
a better, bigger, braver land.

SRH

EN
With thanks to all those who live and work at Petit-Château and all who have helped in the making of these songs.

NL
Met dank aan allen die leven en werken in Klein Kasteeltje en ons hebben geholpen om deze liederen mee vorm te geven.

FR
Merci à tous ceux qui vivent et travaillent au Petit-Château et à tous ceux qui ont contribué à la création de ces chansons.